Washington, DC, Memories

A school group visits the Lincoln
Memorial on a warm spring evening.

Washington, DC, Memories

David Muse

The Countryman Press
Woodstock, Vermont

Book design and composition by Susan McClellan

Published by The Countryman Press, P.O. Box 748,
Woodstock, VT 05091

Distributed by W. W. Norton & Company, Inc.,
500 Fifth Avenue, New York, NY 10110
Printed in China

10 9 8 7 6 5 4 3 2 1

Washington, DC, Memories
978-0-88150-986-1

▶ The twilight skyline
of Washington, DC

Introduction

VACATION—WHAT A WONDERFUL WORD! Eating out, driving around, doing what you want when you want—why does anyone ever go home? Ok, there is that work thing, but life is too short to work all the time. Isn't it time to start planning your next trip, your next fun adventure? Where to this time?

How do your pictures turn out on vacation trips? Do you get some good shots? All nicely sorted and labeled and presented, are they? You must get up early and stay out all day with camera in hand, chasing the best light. Do you wait for those perfect moments, when the action is just right and everything looks perfect?

Well, of course not. You're on vacation! You have better things to do than wake up before dawn and wait around with your camera all day. You have fun all the time and you take pictures when you can. But don't worry! That's why there are professional photographers: somebody has to be out there taking pictures when everyone else is having a good time!

This book is for you, the fun people out there; consider it your personal photo album of the area. Hundreds of miles were driven, hours and hours were spent, and thousands of images were taken over many months to get the best of the best pictures for this book. We might not have taken *every* beautiful picture possible out there, but we believe we got most of them.

If, when looking through this book, you find that a favorite place was left out, I do apologize, but that just means it will stay hidden and private and "yours" a little while longer. If, on the other hand, you'd like to share your photos of favorite spots in this area, I have just the thing for you: Go to www.tcpmemorybooks.com and post your pictures of favorite places that should be included. Think of it as your own online second edition.

I'm thinking the Maine coast, or California's Wine Country or Vail, Colorado, would be good places to go next on vacation. Ready? See you there!

David Middleton, *series editor*

▶ Is this the first squirrel?

◀ The rising sun colors
the sky above the
U.S. Capitol Building.

Washington, DC, Memories

WASHINGTON, DC, IS MANY THINGS TO MANY PEOPLE. It is the nation's capital, seat of the three branches of government; a cultural center, home to dozens of world-class galleries, museums, and theaters; a pro-sports town, where a number of national league teams compete; and a scholarly city, with several top universities. It is a fantastic place to visit, a major U.S. destination for domestic and international travelers alike.

Washington, DC, covers about the same area as New York City, but with only about one third its population. It's a breeze getting around town thanks to public transportation, especially the Metro subway system. DC ranks among the most walkable cities in the U.S. Amble about and enjoy the blend of architectural styles sure to remind you of other times and places.

DC is home to hundreds of memorials, monuments, and statues, too. The most famous, including the new Martin Luther King, Jr. Memorial, are along the National Mall. Near the Mall are other key destinations: the White House, the Supreme Court Building, and the Library of Congress. But DC also has, among others, an Albert Einstein Memorial, a park dedicated to Sonny Bono, and a statue honoring Maine lobstermen. The Mall is also a happening place, hosting such key annual events as the National Cherry Blossom Festival, the Smithsonian Folklife Festival, and the spectacular July 4th fireworks.

Treat yourself to several out-of-the-ordinary museums while you're in town—my favorites include the Newseum, the National Building Museum, and the National Museum of Crime & Punishment. And pay a visit to top-ten destinations outside downtown: among them Arlington National Cemetery, Mount Vernon, the National Cathedral (where Darth Vader is one of the gargoyles!), and the National Zoo.

I encourage you to visit our nation's capital—I do, several times each year, to photograph and to soak up the ambiance. One of my favorite things to do is order a delicious, steaming-fresh hot dog from a street vendor. Look for me on the Mall—I'll be the one with all the camera equipment, enjoying a hot dog smothered in mustard and sauerkraut.

▲ Military band concert on
the steps of the Capitol

◀ The U.S. Capitol on a late
afternoon

◀ *Progress of Civilization*,
sculpted by
Thomas Crawford

▶ A tourist admires the
U.S. Capitol Rotunda.

◀ Twilight at the
other end of
Pennsylvania
Avenue

15

▶ Lafayette Park
sits across
from the
White House.

16

◀ A spring evening at
the White House

Schoolchildren hope for a
glance of the president.

The South Lawn of the White House

◀ The Washington
Monument in
springtime,
viewed from
the Jefferson
Memorial

▶ Enjoying a
spring stroll

Predawn light colors the sky
over Washington, DC

▲ American flags, one for
each U.S. state, surround the
Washington Monument.

▶ A tranquil evening view
along the National Mall

Early spring morning
at the Lincoln Memorial

▶ Predawn view of the
Lincoln Memorial

◀ The rising sun shines
on Lincoln's statue
only during the spring
and summer months.

◀ Canadian
visitors at the
Reflecting Pool
and Lincoln
Memorial

▶ Morning patrol
at the Korean
War Veterans
Memorial

◀ Tourists crowd the
memorial to Thomas
Jefferson, the third
U.S. president.

37

The Rotunda of the
Jefferson Memorial

◀ A quiet moment
together beneath
the cherry trees

◀ Cherry blossom time
in Washington, DC

▶ Capturing the Jefferson
Memorial during the
National Cherry
Blossom Festival

▶ ▶ A Japanese couple in
native costume at the
Cherry Blossom Festival

The Breadline, at the FDR Memorial, is a popular place for photos.

◀ Fireside chat redux . . .
listening to FDR's
radio broadcasts

▶ Neil Estern sculpted
this piece for the
Franklin Delano
Roosevelt Memorial in
Washington, DC.

THEY (WHO) SEEK TO ESTABLISH
STEMS OF GOVERNMENT BASED ON
THE REGIMENTATION OF ALL HUMAN
EINGS BY A HANDFUL OF INDIVIDUAL
RULERS... CALL THIS A NEW ORDER.
T IS NOT NEW AND IT IS NOT ORDER.

◀ People pause to ponder
and photograph the new
Martin Luther King Jr.
National Memorial.

▶ The inscription on the
MLK Memorial reads:
"Out of the mountain of
despair, a stone of hope."

◀ In memory and
honor of fallen
heroes and a
Founding Father

▶ Among the many—
a few of the 58,272
names on the
Vietnam Veterans
Memorial

▶ ▶   Frederick Hart
sculpted this
memorial, known
as the Three
Servicemen Statue.

◀ A group of high school seniors visits the World War II Memorial at twilight.

▶ Early morning
  visitors to the
  WWII Memorial

◀ Late afternoon view
  of the Washington
  Monument from
  the WWII Memorial

◀ A sentinel stands
  guard at the Tomb
  of the Unknowns.

▶ Memorial Day in
  Arlington National
  Cemetery

▶ ▶ The eternal flame
  at President John F.
  Kennedy's gravesite
  in Arlington National
  Cemetery

WASHINGTON, DC, MEMORIES

▲ The gravesite of Pierre L'Enfant,
the architect who designed
Washington, DC

◀ The Women in Military Service
for America Memorial in
Arlington National Cemetery

◀ A young girl asks her mother about the United States Marine Corps War Memorial near Washington, DC.

▶ Into the wild blue yonder—the United States Air Force Memorial

▲ Double-decker tour
buses are a colorful way
to see the city.

▲ *Beep-beep!*
Sightseeing along
the National Mall
via City Segway Tours.

▲ With DC Ducks you
can tour the Capitol
by land and by water.

▶ Washington's Union
  Station is a central
  hub for Amtrak and
  the Metro Red Line.

◀ The DC Metro subway
  system is the second
  busiest in the country,
  after New York City's.

The Enid A. Haupt Garden brightens
the grounds of the Smithsonian Castle.

◀ The original
Smithsonian Museum
is known as the Castle.

▶ Joseph Henry was
the first secretary
of the Smithsonian
Institution.

WASHINGTON, DC, MEMORIES

▶ Calm waters—
a reflection of the
National Museum of
the American Indian

◀ Choctaw Nation
dancers at the
National Museum
of the American
Indian

◀ *Typewriter Eraser*, by Claes Oldenburg in the Sculpture Garden at the National Gallery of Art

▶ A visitor to the National Air and Space Museum marvels at the Skylab 4 command module.

▶ ▶ The moon rock in the National Air and Space Museum is nearly 4 billion years old.

▶ America by Air—
a major exhibit in
the National Air
and Space Museum

Discovery Station

Discovery Station

We
to the Ele

Trunk raised,
ears fanned...
this elephant is
his attention, an

In this Museum, w
using our rich colle
of nature and cultu

Come join this invest
Explore this small slic
and the many exhibits

▶ The Rotunda of the
Smithsonian National
Museum of Natural
History and its
iconic pachyderm

◀ Father and son
are dwarfed by the
African elephant
in the Smithsonian
National Museum
of Natural History.

Ruby slippers from
The Wizard of Oz
1938

▲ There's no place like home ...

◄ Mysterious beauty—the famous Hope Diamond

▲ Enjoying a game
near the Washington
Monument.

▲ Just the thing for a hot
summer day.

▲ One is likely to see a
softball game along the
National Mall on a
summer evening.

◀ The Five Amigos, a Colombian singing group, at the Smithsonian Folklife Festival

▶ One entry in the Blossom Kite Festival takes flight along the National Mall.

▶ ▶ Future soccer star

◀ Yes, he's juggling a basketball, a tennis racket, and a bowling ball!

▶ A modern minstrel entertains along the National Mall.

▶ ▶ Enjoying delicious treats on the Mall

WASHINGTON, DC, MEMORIES

85

▲ A winged figurehead represents Discovery on
the Christopher Columbus Memorial Fountain.

▶ The fountain, designed
by Lorado Taft,
features a 15-foot-tall
statue of Columbus.

◀ Late afternoon in front
of the Supreme Court

A pair of statues sit
before the Supreme
Court building,
*Contemplation of
Justice* (left) and
Authority of Law
(right).

◀ Minerva, the goddess
of learning and
wisdom, in the Great
Hall of the Library
of Congress.

▶ Another view of the
Great Hall showcases
the arches, stonework,
and artwork.

A monumental view from
the Old Post Office Tower

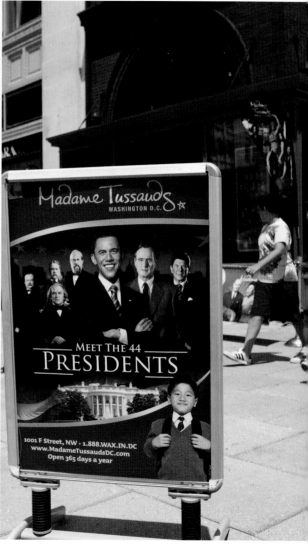

WASHINGTON, DC, MEMORIES

▶ A statue of Ben
Franklin stands before
the Old Post Office.

◀ A presidential
gathering at Madame
Tussauds wax museum.

◀ ◀ The site of
President Lincoln's
assassination still
operates as a theater.

◀ The delightful interior of the National Building Museum

▶ A multilevel view of the Newseum

▶ ▶ Outside the National Portrait Gallery

▶ At the Newseum a
  visitor photographs
  artwork painted by
  Indiano on the former
  Berlin Wall.

◀ A twisted radio tower
  from the World Trade
  Center is on display
  at the Newseum in
  memory of 9/11.

Early morning view of Mount Vernon,
George and Martha Washington's home

▲ View of the Washington
National Cathedral, the sixth
largest cathedral in the world,
from Bishop's Garden

▶ One stained-glass window in the National
Cathedral depicts George Washington.

▶ ▶ Seemingly endless, the National Cathedral's
center aisle is as long as two football fields.

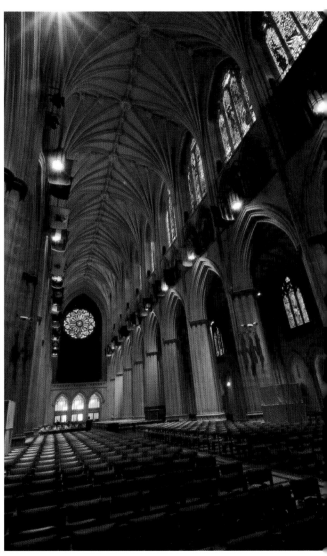

▲ I ❤ DC souvenir
shop at the Old
Post Office Pavillion

▲ Cool sunglasses,
by George

▲ Duke Ellington mural on
the True Reformer Building
in Washington's U Street
neighborhood

◀ Colorful rowhouses
in the Adams Morgan
neighborhood

▶ Madam's Organ Blues
Bar, in the heart of
the Adams Morgan
neighborhood

▶ ▶ Marilyn Monroe
watches over the
Woodley Park
neighborhood.

110 WASHINGTON. DC. MEMORIES

▲ One of the most popular
residents of the National
Aquarium

◀ Family members share
an affectionate moment
at the National Zoo.

◀ A summer-camp group visiting the National Zoo poses at the main entrance.